SINCERE

CONDOLENCES

What to Say When You
Don't Know What to Say

JOYCE AITKEN

◆ FriesenPress

Suite 300 - 990 Fort St
Victoria, BC, V8V 3K2
Canada

www.friesenpress.com

ISBN
978-1-5255-7813-7 (Hardcover)
978-1-5255-7814-4 (Paperback)
978-1-5255-7815-1 (eBook)

1. FAMILY & RELATIONSHIPS, DEATH, GRIEF, BEREAVEMENT

Distributed to the trade by The Ingram Book Company

In Memory of
Gordon Donald Aitken
1959–2016

I've heard it said
That people come into our lives for a reason
Bringing something we must learn
And we are led
To those who help us most to grow
And if we let them
And if we help them in return
Well, I don't know if I believe that's true
But I know I'm who I am today
Because I knew you ...

So much of me
Is made of what I learned from you
You'll be with me
Like a handprint on my heart

Who can say if I've been changed for
the better?
I do believe I've been changed for the better
And because I knew you ...
Because I knew you ...
I have been changed for good ...

For Good
Kristin Chenoweth, Idina Menzel

CONTENTS

INTRODUCTION

HAS THIS EVER HAPPENED TO YOU?

A RELATIVE, FRIEND, COLLEAGUE OR MEMBER OF YOUR community has suffered the tragic loss of a loved one. You immediately rush to see them, because you know exactly what to say and do to bring them comfort in this situation.

If that is you, then congratulations! You are in a very small minority.

Most of us can find suitable expressions of sympathy when someone's elderly grandparent passes away after a long, meaningful life. Most of us have probably had that sort of personal grief experience. It's a natural part of life. We know that people don't live forever. We certainly

1

deeply mourn the loss of beloved parents and grandparents, but as people age, their ability to enjoy life is often lessened as they deal with illness or age-related difficulties. Even though we dearly love them, it is sometimes a relief when their suffering is over and we consider them to be free from the burdens of this world. This type of grief is a normal, natural-cycle-of-life type of grief that may leave us with ongoing feelings of sadness for some time. We miss these people in our lives but we find it easy to be comforted by our memories of them. We are not generally burdened with questions of how and why they could have possibly died.

The grief I am talking about in this book is the result of an **unexpected, tragic, out-of- time, life-altering loss.** The type of loss that completely changes the trajectory of our life; the type of loss from which our nightmares are made.

Most of us, gratefully, travel through life with a rather myopic view of grief. Generally, it's a topic that most of us prefer to avoid any in-depth contemplation about until we are actually faced with the reality of tragic loss. When suddenly confronted with the need to respond to tragedy, most of us tend to feel lost and completely inadequate. We genuinely *want* to be able to provide comfort, but we worry that we may actually worsen a difficult situation by saying or doing the wrong thing.

In 2016, my life changed forever when my wonderful husband, Gordon, took his life at the age of fifty-six. In a million years, anyone who knew him could not have imagined this happening. He suffered from what I now know was high-functioning depression or persistent depressive disorder. At the time, I thought he had what I would characterize as "occasional blue spells." It did not seem to visibly interfere with his work or life, and his depression was not noticeable to anyone. He kept his anguish completely inside and worked diligently at putting forward what appeared to all the world to be a very "normal" persona. When people saw him, they always saw his 1000-watt smile and his quick, cheerful wit. In fact, when most people heard of his death, they simply couldn't believe it. Surely someone had gotten their wires crossed with that news. His death was a seismic shock to our family, our friends and our community.

This book is a result of my experiences as family, friends and community rallied to be of comfort. It's a compilation of wonderful experiences and also some difficult experiences. What was overwhelmingly apparent was the absolute desire of people to "do" something, combined with some insecurity in knowing what this "doing" would or could look like. Since the loss of my husband, people often ask me for suggestions in regard to what they could do to support someone who has suddenly experienced profound, life-altering loss.

There is no personal exemption from grief. Either you have already known someone whose life has been altered by tragic loss, or you inevitably will—and when you do, this book may be of assistance to you. Hopefully, it will give you the confidence to respond in a manner that is both helpful and compassionate.

FIRST,

A WORD ABOUT NORTH AMERICAN GRIEF CULTURE

EVERYONE WHO IS BORN EVENTUALLY DIES. THERE IS NO other possible outcome. Having said that, our understanding of grief, which affects literally every human being, is extremely limited. Most of us spend little time contemplating grief until we are actually touched by it. Generally, when it does touch us, while we are very sympathetic to people's pain and suffering, we are inherently uncomfortable with it. We just want it to go away.

We live in a cultural narrative of grief denial. We see it as a problem to be resolved, a malady that needs to be "cured." We want people to get over their grief and get back to normal, whatever that is. We're caught up in our first-world attitude of instant gratification/instant fix/ take a pill and be better in the morning. Studies have shown that, on average, we have sympathy for bereaved people for about three months. After that, we tend to forget that they are grieving. If we witness them behaving in a way that we would consider outside of normal, getting-it-all-together type behavior, then we think either a) some new unfortunate event must have happened in their life; or b) they are stuck in grief, which sounds a lot like a judgment, indicating that they have somehow failed at getting over grief.

Many people are familiar with the work of Dr. Elizabeth Kübler-Ross, who introduced denial, anger, bargaining, depression and acceptance as the five stages of grief in her 1969 book *On Death and Dying*. The wider population came to believe that these were the five definitive stages of grief that people went through in something of a lineal progression, with a view to being "through" grief once they were completed. This was definitely not Dr. Kübler-Ross' intent. The stages were clearly intended to be descriptive NOT prescriptive. In current thinking, the stages are now thought of as something that people may or may not experience. If they do, it's unlikely the stages will be in any lineal order.

Grief is now starting to be understood in a way that anyone who has suffered intense grief could have told us. The reality is, we do not get **through** or **over** grief. Rather, we **adapt** to its presence in our lives. It changes us forever and will be with us forever. There is no magic formula, no pill, no cure, no words of such comfort that they make everything all right. It takes much, much, much longer than most people realize for people to move from intense grief to assimilating the grief into their life in a way that allows them to manage it. Grief is the malaria of emotions. It will always be there, and people may experience lifelong reoccurring flares of intense grief from time to time.

The reality is this: cataclysmic, life-altering loss simply cannot be fixed or made better in any way. It can only be **endured.** This is not to say that people live the rest of their lives in intense grief. We do not. We simply would not be able to survive that level of pain permanently. We are not hardwired to stay in intense grief forever.

People find healing from their initial shock and despair in a number of ways. Survivors of loss do manage to go on to live lives that can be rewarding and even joyful. New and meaningful plans and dreams can eventually be made. But grief will always be part of the new life. Always.

What we can't do is replace the person who is lost to us forever in this world. There is simply no making that right. That is the loss that will be part of our life forever.

That is the absolute truth.

WHAT DOES GRIEF
FEEL LIKE?

THE FIRST STEP IN BEING ABLE TO RESPOND EFFECTIVELY
to someone's grief situation is to develop some understanding of what grief is actually like.

Many people are familiar with the metaphor of grief as a
shipwreck. Here is one version found on social media and
attributed to some anonymous wise, elderly gentleman.

I find this description to be one of the most profoundly
accurate descriptions of grief:

> *Grief is like a shipwreck. When the ship is first*
> *wrecked, you're drowning, with wreckage all*
> *around you. Everything floating around you*
> *reminds you of the beauty and magnificence*
> *of the ship that was and is no more. All you*

*can do is float. You find some piece of wreckage
and you hang on for awhile. Maybe it's some
physical thing. Maybe it's a happy memory or a
photograph. Maybe it's another person who's also
floating. For awhile all you can do is float. Stay
alive. In other words, just hang on.*

*In the beginning, the waves are a hundred feet
tall and crash over you without mercy. They come
ten seconds apart and don't even give you time to
catch your breath. All you can do is hang on and
float. After a while, maybe weeks, maybe months,
you'll find the waves are still a hundred feet tall
but they come further apart. When they come, they
still crash all over you and wipe you out. But in
between, you can breathe, you can start to function
a bit. You never know what's going to trigger
the grief. It might be a song, a picture, a street
intersection, the smell of a cup of coffee. It can be
anything, and the wave comes crashing. But in
between waves, eventually there is life.*

*Somewhere down the line, and it's different for
everybody, you find that the waves are only eighty
feet tall. Or fifty feet tall. And while they still
come, they come further apart. You can see them*

coming. An anniversary, a birthday, Christmas,
or landing at Heathrow. You can see it coming for
the most part, and prepare yourself. And when it
washes over you, you know that somehow you will
come out the other side. Soaking wet, sputtering,
still holding on to some tiny piece of the wreckage,
but you'll come out.

There will always be waves. For those who have lost someone they deeply love, their particular sea will never be devoid of waves.

This book is intended to provide some ideas for lifelines amid those waves. Lifelines that you can throw out to someone who is floating on that sea of despair.

LIFELINE 1

REACH OUT

IF WE ARE HONEST, COMPLETELY HONEST, WHEN SOME horrible tragedy strikes someone's family, our preferred option would probably be to leave the country to avoid encountering the survivors. Let's face it, this type of a visit where we enter into someone else's pain is extremely difficult.

There are two categories of "reaching out."

First, there are people whom you have a relationship with that you know that you simply must go see. Second, there are those for whom it would be inappropriate to show up on their doorstep, but you definitely need to communicate with them.

Of course, if the loss is someone in your family, you will be there as soon as possible. When the loss is anyone else, there are two important reasons to reach out to that person or family as soon as possible:

1) If you put off reaching out to people who have experienced tragedy, the task becomes more difficult. The first encounter with people is always the most difficult. Once you have that behind you, it will be much easier. If you put it off, you run the risk of running into them unexpectedly, when you are unprepared, and your handling of that situation may not go as you want it to.

2) When my husband died, I initially felt that the grief was so unbearable that I would not be able to survive it. I was inundated with messages from people near and far. The sheer number of messages that I received had a very profound effect. I remember having a strong sense that the community was going to hold me, lift me up and support me until I could stand on my own. The power of messages, or prayers, if that is your comfort, or just the good energy of others holding you in their thoughts is very uplifting. It has a synergistic effect. A single message is helpful, but having many, many people

holding you in their thoughts is greater than the sum of its parts. It's very powerful.

Reach out as soon as you can.

If you are able to go see people, by all means do it. If you are in doubt about whether you should go see them, just do it—briefly. Chances are they have someone who is doing a bit of gatekeeping to control the flow of visitors, and this person may tell you if it is a good time for a visit.

We live in a world of instant communication. If you are unable to see them, by all means text or message them. All messages are valuable. You may or may not get a reply, but your message will be appreciated.

Sometimes what happens is you run into bereaved people unexpectedly before you have had a chance to go see them. When this happens, the bereaved can almost read your mind. When they see the surprised look on your face, they know that you are thinking:

> "OMG, I didn't expect to see Susan today.
> Her husband was just killed yesterday!
> What on earth is she doing out?
> I'm not emotionally prepared for this!

I haven't figured out what to say yet!
I'm just going to pretend I didn't see her
and wait until I'm more prepared."

It seems that, when tragedy strikes, people have a perception that the survivors move to a cave, never to be seen in the light of day until much later. In reality, grief-stricken people still occasionally have to go out, and it sometimes shocks people to see them at the gas station, grocery store or doctor's office. Often, in this situation, people panic and make the unfortunate decision to pretend they didn't see the bereaved person. Come on, admit it. Most of us have acted in this way at some time, and it's easy to justify by telling yourself you're just not up to this difficult encounter at this time, or you're running late for your tap-dancing lesson, or you're not emotionally strong during this phase of the lunar cycle. Unfortunately, when this happens, the bereaved person almost always notices that someone is pretending not to see them. It makes them feel victimized and is just another hurtful experience at an already painful time. Don't do this! Just acknowledge the person in a simple way.

Forget about madly searching for something profound to say. "I'm so sorry" are the most important words, and all that is necessary. I once had someone come up to me who was clearly shocked at seeing me unexpectedly and simply didn't know what to say. The person clasped their hands and bowed to me in the typical "Namaste" greeting. It was heartfelt. It was sincere. It was all that was needed.

- **Reach out as soon as possible by personal visit, text message or phone call**

- **It's very comforting for survivors to know immediately that others are holding them in their thoughts**

- **Always acknowledge bereaved people if you run into them unexpectedly**

LIFELINE 2

DON'T WORRY ABOUT WHAT TO SAY

WE ALL WANT TO COME UP WITH THE ONE PIECE OF PRO-
found wisdom that will lift the person out of the abyss
of despair. The reality is that there are no words that will
work that magic. There is really nothing that you can say.
NOTHING. Of course, this goes completely against the
grain of our societal predisposition for fast-fix cures of all
problems. We have the mindset that the coins of the realm,
when visiting a grieving person, are to provide words of
comfort and **empathy**. Metaphorically, we do not want
to show up empty handed when we go to visit someone.

Remember, the three most powerful words are: "I'm
so sorry." When we visit someone in intense grief, the

comfort is in our presence, not in our words. Grieving people just need others to comfort them by **acknowledging** their horrific grief. Just sitting with them. Bearing witness to them. They do not need anyone to try to fix it or rationalize it.

They may need someone to listen to their story. The telling of the story repeatedly is sometimes a way that helps our brains start to accept the reality of the unacceptable. They may need to talk, talk, talk about it. You only need to listen. Or, people in intense grief may not be able to talk about it at all. It's hard for us to sit in radio silence. We're unaccustomed to it. This is not a time to fill the silence with mindless prattle. If they don't want to talk, just ask if it would be alright to sit quietly with them for a short time.

I repeat: **your presence is the comfort, not your words.** The fact is that even if you were able to come up with some wise, profound, enlightening message, it's highly unlikely the grieving family would even be able to remember it. Grief will likely have obliterated their ability to retain conversations. I have memories of people coming and going in my home in the days following my husband's death. I remember them preparing or delivering food, doing dishes and all manner of helpful things. I have little recollection of any conversations. It really does render unimportant any concern you have over what to say.

Even if you have experienced a similar loss, no one can completely understand how anyone else feels about their loss. There's an expression that the worst grief in the world is your own. While there is no point to comparing grief experiences, there is a hierarchy to grief. The loss of a loved one is not the same as someone's loss of their beloved family pet or their disappointment over losing their job or their daughter's devastation over not getting accepted into the college of her choice. These are certainly losses that people grieve, but they are not in the realm of the death of a person you love. Please resist any temptation to compare.

Kelsey Crowe and Emily McDowell have developed a brilliant line of greeting cards, and my favourite reads *"When life gives you lemons, I won't tell you a story about my cousin's friend who died of lemons."*

A rather surprising experience I had during my initial grief was people telling me intimate, private, personal information. I can only place this in the category of: **"You're Not**

the Only Person Whose Life Sucks Right Now." My speculation is that the sharing of this information was somehow meant to encourage me by highlighting the universality of suffering. These revelations of marital difficulties, financial distress, addictions and family discord were simply confusing to me. At a time when shock and despair rendered me unable to remember what day it was, I simply could not process anyone else's misery, and it only added to the overload of my brain. In fact, the brain fog I was under usually left me wondering months later if I had heard that news, dreamt it, or where it originated.

Sometimes what people say when trying to comfort you sounds like rationalization. It sounds like they feel you shouldn't be in such deep despair over your loved one's death because:

- *It's Part of God's Plan*

  Please, please, please leave God out of this! All that statement does is make me mad at God (if I wasn't already). Even the most faithful adherents may experience some crisis of faith in the wake of devastating loss. Regardless of what the person's faith tradition is, the subject of where God, Allah, Buddha, or their spiritual unicorn guide was in this tragedy is a subject best left to the person's own trusted spiritual advisor. Tragedy often leads people to intense esoteric self-examination of their belief system. Trust me, they will sort it out on their own. If they specifically request your spiritual opinion on the matter, then that is different story, but please don't casually throw out these "God" statements. Conversely, the grieving person may say something such as "The only thing keeping me from losing my mind is knowing this must be part of God's plan." It's fine for someone in grief to say that. It's not helpful for anyone else to express it.

- *God Must Have Needed Another Angel*
  Seriously?

- *God Only Takes the Best*
  What? The worst of humankind get to live forever?

- *God Works in All Things for Good*
  I will never, never, never see that this is good!

- *God Never Gives You More Than You Can Handle*

So, this is my fault? If I were weaker, this wouldn't have happened?

- *You Were So Lucky to Have Them for the Time You Did*
  Somehow I'm not feeling lucky right now.

- *They're in a Better Place*
  This place was pretty wonderful. I want them in this place, not some unknown place.

- *This Really Makes You Understand What's Important in Life*
  Thanks, but I already knew that.

- *Wait and See! This Will Be a Transformational Experience for You*
  My life was pretty wonderful. I did not need for my husband to die, and he did not deserve to die so I could be transformed to living some higher purpose life.

- *You Agreed to This in a Previous Lifetime*
  That might be an interesting concept to discuss, but it provides zero comfort to a grieving person at this time.

A useful practice is to mentally run your comforting thoughts through the sieve of rationalization before saying them out loud. If the thought gets hung up on the "but," as in "This is tragic, **but** . . .," best to keep that thought to yourself.

When you summon the courage to visit someone who has just experienced tragedy, resist trying to "fix." Just be present to their pain. Just be present.

Of course, it goes without saying that people need to be sincere in whatever they say. I'm particularly uncomfortable with the casual use of the expression "How are you?" and I would love to see it obliterated from our communal zeitgeist. You know how this goes. You meet someone you know on your way out of a store and they say, "Hey, how are ya?" Before you even think of answering, the person is already inside the store, with no real interest in actually having a discussion on how you are. The expression has become a meaningless salutation.

It becomes a cringe-worthy moment when it's directed to a grieving person. Many times I've wanted to say, "My husband's dead, how do you think I am?" when I've been on the receiving end of an uber-casual "How are ya." If

I were to answer with any honesty, I would have to say something like: "*Well, I'm consumed with sadness, despair, helplessness and hopelessness. I'm lonely and depressed, and most days I feel like I'm losing my mind. I can't sleep and I'm unable to make the simplest of decisions. The brain fog I'm mired in has made it impossible for me to recall your name, even though I know I have known you for fifteen years. Other than that, I'm fine.*" It's so much better to just say hello or ask how someone is doing **today**.

- **The comfort is in your presence, not in your words**

- **Don't try to FIX**

- **Don't rationalize the loss**

- **Don't compare losses**

- **It's not the time to talk about your own problems**

- **Just be present**

LIFELINE 3

NEVER FEAR TEARS

MANY OF US HAVE AN IRRATIONAL FEAR OF TEARS. WE
don't want to be responsible for making someone cry. I've
often heard someone say something like, "I just feel terrible. I made a comment to Mary about Joe's passing and
it made her cry." First off, Mary is not crying because of
something the person said. Mary is crying because Joe is
dead, plain and simple. *Tears often mean little to the person
shedding them.* When people are in grief, tears are as much
a part of their normal existence as breathing. Many grieving people cry so frequently that they don't even notice it
anymore. Seldom, bordering on never, are we concerned
about tears when our life has been completely shattered.
Tears are a healing release. Grieving people are generally
not disturbed by tears; unfortunately, others are.

The best emotional analogy I can come up with is that of a **pressure cooker**. When we are in our deepest grief, we are completely consumed by loss, anguish and despair. It's always, always, there, subcutaneously, barely below the surface at all times, building pressure. When we are able to release tears, it actually releases the pressure of these overwhelming emotions. In many ways, it's a cleansing release.

Societally, we are expected to shape up and look like we are getting it all together. We know that our continued pain and anguish makes others uncomfortable, especially as it goes on longer than people expect. So when we are out and about, we feel compelled to put on our "I'm okay" face. This is often a false face. If it's been some time since our loss, people just don't want to see us crying in the tomatoes at the grocery store. This constant effort to wear the "I'm okay" face when we step outside our home builds up incredible pressure inside us. It's exhausting and difficult. In some other cultures, grief traditions dictate that people wear black armbands for a period of a year after a loss. This signals to the public that this person is in mourning and therefore there is an altered expectation of their behavior. We could benefit from this tradition in our grief-denial culture in much of North America.

About six months after my husband passed, I stopped to pick up my mail in my rural post office. Gathering up several pieces of mail addressed to my husband completely overwhelmed me and I stood in the post office weeping profusely. A casual acquaintance came along and said, "Oh no, what's wrong, has something happened?" I wanted to scream, "YES, MY HUSBAND IS DEAD!!" which, of course, this person knew. It simply highlights the great divide between how fresh the grief still was to me and how this person thought I should be well beyond public displays of despair. The black armband would have been helpful.

The best response to someone's tears is to try not to be unduly disturbed by them. Don't let fear of "upsetting" someone hold you back from talking to them. Crying is the release valve on our pressure-cooker emotions. Crying is good. It means little to the grieving person. Get comfortable with it.

- **Do not be concerned about tears**

- **Tears often mean little to those in grief**

- **Tears relieve emotional pressure and are a cleansing release**

LIFELINE 4

IT'S NEVER TOO LATE

WE ALL HAVE BUSY LIVES. HAVE YOU EVER INTENDED TO send someone a sympathy card but it slipped your mind, and then you felt too much time had passed to send it?

It's never too late.

Time stands still for those in grief when the loss is life-altering. A message of condolence is always welcome, even years later.

Never underestimate the value of cards and notes. When my husband passed, I received literally hundreds of cards and letters. I went through them several times in the early days after his funeral. Several years later, I went through them all again. A box of Kleenex later, I felt like I was wrapped in a warm hug of comfort from these cards and letters. After the passage of time, I was able to fully appreciate the carefully chosen images, words and heartfelt messages in the cards. I found that I had received cards I had no recollection of receiving, due to the brain fog of grief in the early days. People may keep condolence cards and letters for quite some time, and they can be an ongoing source of comfort.

One of my very thoughtful friends continued to send me cards regularly for over a year after my husband passed. They always contained a "Thinking of you" message. It was uncanny how often these cards arrived when the ongoing weight of grief was threatening to sink me. The restorative value of these messages was huge. The knowledge that someone else was intentionally holding our family in their ongoing thoughts was such a boost of encouragement.

It's easy enough to send a card or message at any time. Consider doing it many months after someone's loss. Just do it. I always have a box of sympathy cards on hand as well as a box of blank "Thinking of you" cards. When I write out a sympathy card, I often write out a few "Thinking of you" cards and leave them on my desk with notes to send a few months later. It's a good reminder to myself later that this person is still very much in need of compassionate support. The act of sending physical cards and letters has become something of a lost art. Pity. I know from personal experience that receiving a card will provide ongoing encouragement to a person for many days as it sits on their counter or posted on their fridge. It really is a small act that takes relatively small effort but has huge, lasting impact.

"Do small things with great love"
– Mother Teresa

- It's **NEVER** too late to send condolences

- Cards and letters are an ongoing source of comfort

LIFELINE 5

RESPECT ENERGY

GRIEF TAKES ENERGY, AND INTENSE GRIEF TAKES ALMOST all a person's energy. This is why someone in intense grief might be able to eat something if food is placed before them, but they may not be able to have enough energy to prepare food.

It's thought that intense grief can take over 90% of a person's energy, leaving little left for anything else. As time goes on, the energy required for grief will wax and wane, leaving the person able to do other things, but this ability can be very transient. A person can feel up to doing something but suddenly, without warning, their energy is completely depleted.

It's important to understand the energy matrix of grief. It will help you understand why someone may say they can or will do something, but suddenly they simply can't.

Grief counsellors cautioned me many times about how grief affects our energy, but I was a very slow learner. I am normally a high-energy person. My idling speed revs fairly high, and I've never had to consider that I might not have enough energy to complete a task. I do contractual work that often requires me to travel several hours from home. In the months following my husband's death, I took on a lot of work in an effort to try to provide myself with enough distraction to survive the days. I could generally summon enough energy to arrive at the destination and do several hours of work, only to then find myself sitting crying on the side of the road without sufficient energy to drive home. This total depletion of energy can sneak up on a person without warning. I would speculate that most people would struggle with energy depletion for at least a year, possibly much longer, after tragedy or a very difficult death.

Certainly for the first year, our energy goes to what we need to do to survive. My personal survival plan that I maintained for well after a year was to make a list each night of three things I would do the next day. This was not a list of life goals. My list generally looked something like: "Make coffee, feed the cat, wash my hair." The list was ground zero for me. It forced me to summon the energy to do something. Without this commitment to myself, I would sit for hours each day, immobilized in my rocking chair.

I had a conversation with an acquaintance who was ranting about her cousin, who had lost her spouse six months earlier. She was doing her best to be helpful by arranging many activities for her cousin to "get her mind off her grief." She said her cousin always said she would go to these various activities with her but often cancelled at the last minute. My acquaintance said, "You know, she's just gotten so lazy since her husband died." Yikes! There may be many reasons for the cousin's cancellations, but lazy probably didn't factor into it. Energy could quite likely be at the top of the list. It's not possible to predict your energy in advance, and it's difficult for people to understand that if they haven't experienced grief-filled energy depletion themselves.

Be kind if people have to back out of planned activities. Sometimes, it takes all the energy reserves a person possesses just to survive.

- **Keep in mind that grief is an enormous drain of people's energy**

- **Understand that energy is unpredictable, and grieving people often need to cancel plans**

LIFELINE 6

WONDERFUL WORLD
OF DISTRACTION

WHEN SOMEONE HAS LOST A SIGNIFICANT PERSON, THEIR life becomes unrecognizable to them. Nothing makes sense or feels real. The only way I can describe it is that it seems like you are in an altered universe, with no ability whatsoever to find your North Star. It takes a long, long time for people to find and adjust to their "new normal."

In the meantime, **distraction** is a wonderful thing. Distraction will not make the person forget their loss (not even for a second). It will, however, fill in some time while they are trying to come to terms with their new reality. There is a surreal sense of being in limbo after the loss of a loved one. You don't want a new life; you want your old one. You can't even comprehend your new reality. You have limited ability to think clearly. Time simply has to pass and pass and pass and pass...........

It's a wonderful gift when people help you through these limbo days with some distraction. Anything can be helpful, keeping in mind the energy matrix. The best plans are ones that have an escape route, such as taking the person somewhere with an assurance that they can be brought home whenever they wish, no questions asked.

There is no need to feel that you have to plan a big event or outing to entertain someone. Invite them to go for coffee, for a walk, a drive, to watch a movie, or to keep you company as you do something. Anything that distracts the person for even a short time from their solitary world of trying to adjust to their loss.

My husband passed away in the spring of 2016. Later that year, the US elected their forty-fifth president, which probably created unprecedented political dialogue in North America and around the world. Had my husband been alive, we, too, would have had much conversation about this sensational election. As it was, I had zero interest in the current events of the world. Grief shrinks our world into a tiny little box of survival of the moment. My friends and family, however, insisted on discussing the election with me. This discussion was both unimportant and of immense value to me: unimportant in that I just couldn't summon much interest in what was going on in the world at a time when my world was shattered, and immensely valuable in that it did provide distraction for the moments that we engaged in discussion.

Keep engaging people who are bereaved in conversations about interesting topics, even if they are less than enthusiastic conversationalists in return. The diversion is welcome, even if it's not readily apparent.

The first year, of course, is hell as you face all the dreaded "firsts." Unfortunately, these things don't magically get easier after the first year. People associate the "firsts" with the big events, such as birthdays, anniversaries, Christmas. In reality, the firsts are more than the big events. They are also an endless stream of experiences, large and small, that need to be re-navigated.

Every time I left the farm for the afternoon and came back to it being completely as I left it. No vehicles had moved , nothing changed whatsoever. Every time felt like a "first," as I was again confronted with the reality that my spouse was gone.

The first time you attend *any* event by yourself, or do *anything* that you previously would have done together, is a huge emotional challenge. Offering to accompany someone is so helpful. Often, people feel that if an activity is something you regularly do, and that the people in attendance are familiar to you, it will be easy for you to resume. It is not. In my experience the act of walking through the door by yourself is an emotional overload that can hit like a ton of bricks. Attending familiar activities and events can be a huge grief trigger that can take many months to become comfortable with once more. It can be a constant reminder of happier times and a highlight of the overwhelming loss in your life. Again, companionship is the best you can offer for any situation.

Do not assume that if a grieving person wants you to accompany them to an event they will ask. They likely will not. Many people would rather stay home than ask someone to accompany them. At a time when they are so vulnerable, it can feel somewhat desperate. I'm not talking about big events. Even attending small, regular church, sports, or social events of any kind is easier to navigate if someone accompanies you.

> - **Providing any type of diversion to people trying to adjust to a new normal is extremely helpful and appreciated**
>
> - **Offer to accompany or sit with someone at an event**

LIFELINE 7

DO SOMETHING USEFUL

WHEN MY HUSBAND DIED, I WAS LEFT ALONE ON A FARM with a livestock operation that I had little ability to manage. I was not the farmer. I had my own career. I was completely overwhelmed by anything to do with the farm operation and was heavily reliant on family and neighbours to assist me. Since I had to rely on them for the big stuff, I certainly did not want to call them every time I encountered some small thing I couldn't deal with on my own. This happened frequently. As is true with many couples, there were tasks that my husband alone took care of and other tasks that were specifically within my domain.

I like to think that I'm a fairly competent person. My entire career was in management positions, and I'm generally a good problem solver. I've always had a philosophy of looking at failures of any kind as an opportunity to learn from mistakes, to do better next time.

There is however, simply no do-over with death. It is the final frontier. There is nothing that you can do to make the outcome different. The reality of this finality immobilizes you in a way nothing else can.

In addition, the accompanying brain fog of grief can rob you of your confidence and ability to figure anything out or make the simplest decision. I felt as though I morphed overnight from a reasonably competent person to a useless slug that was a terrible burden on others. One of my neighbours got into the wonderful habit of stopping in often when he was driving by, with an inquiry " was there was anything I needed a hand with that day?" YES! I would never phone someone to say, "I can't get my lawnmower started," but since he was there, I was very grateful for this help. I knew I needed help with the big things. It's the small, sniveling, day-to-day things that you've never had to deal with before that leave you feeling completely defeated.

Virtually every person who offered me their condolences said "call me if there's anything I can do to help." These offers were made out of genuine, sincere kindness. Other people were much more specific and intentional in their offers of assistance, asking if they could come and weed the garden, mow the lawn, pick up my mail, shop for groceries and so on. These offers conveyed such earnest desire to be helpful that when I did need specific assistance, I would generally ask one of those people.

In the words of Kahlil Gibran, "The smallest deed is better than the greatest intention."

If you want to be helpful, really helpful, offer to do something specific, and if you can anticipate what someone might need, you definitely win the bonus round. One of the problems is that people in intense grief have limited ability to anticipate anything themselves. They are strictly in the moment, trying to survive.

Some suggestions:

- Instead of saying "Can I bring dinner over sometime?" say "Can I bring dinner over on Wednesday?"
- Offer to do specific yard tasks such as mowing, watering, snow removal

- Pick up some groceries or their mail

- Run errands. Say: "I am going to the drugstore.Is there anything that you need that I could pick up for you?"

- Offer to write thank-you notes or return casserole dishes

- Just **ask** if there is something specific you could do. There may be something they are worrying about but are reluctant to ask for help

Take a look at the person's life and consider what might be particularly difficult:

- Do they have kids that need to be driven to sports or other activities?

- Do they have an elder in their life that needs support?

When you have a huge loss in your life, every aspect of daily life becomes a challenge. To start with, you may be surrounded by family and friends who help you through the initial days. Eventually, everyone has to leave. Eventually, you have to go it on your own. These are the darkest of days.

Loneliness is everything it's cracked up to be. Grief is very lonely business. When you are used to sharing your life with someone who is no longer there, the weight of this loneliness is crushing. Some of the loneliest times in my day have been mealtimes. No matter how busy we were, my husband and I enjoyed sharing our day with each other at mealtime. Preparing a meal to sit at the table and eat by myself is a grief trigger that, to this day, is difficult to overcome. One of the most appreciated gifts has been when someone has invited me to share a simple meal with them. A bowl of soup in the company of someone can feel like an incredible blessing .

I have a wonderful friend Kathy who would often casually call and say, "I'm just making some omelets for a quick supper, why don't you pop over and join us." I couldn't get there fast enough. This was one of the best types of invitation. What it said was: Don't dress up, don't bring anything, don't worry about whether you will feel up to doing this in an hour, just **come now and be however you are**. It also meant that I hadn't inconvenienced them. They hadn't pulled out all the stops to make a "special" meal for a guest. They hadn't spent the day cleaning their house to impress. Sliding my feet under their table and sharing their food and friendship was like slipping into a warm bath. Sitting at their table having a regular weeknight meal and normal family conversation was such a welcome brief reprieve from the cloak of loneliness and sorrow that was my constant companion.

I've had this conversation with many other people who have experienced tragic loss. We are so socialized around food; it becomes for many people a huge stumbling block to eat all of our meals solo. If anyone asked how we are making out with meals, we would probably say we are doing okay, because we feel obliged to tell people what they want to hear and an unwillingness to tell people how much we are struggling with the simple task of feeding ourselves. Few of us are willing to admit that we can barely organize a sandwich. The very act of shopping for groceries can be unmanageable. For a long period of time, I found myself unable to cope with the concentration and decision-making that grocery shopping required. I would end up throwing random items in my cart that were of little use in actually putting a meal together. In addition, coming face to face with ordinary items such as your loved one's favourite tea or snacks or the cheese they really enjoyed can be a powerful grief trigger. Food is one of the most helpful things that people can offer. Everyone needs to eat, and eating with others feeds more than our physical bodies. It really can lift you from the abyss for a short period, particularly in the first year after loss.

A really helpful gesture would be to take someone some pre-made meals or a hamper of food items a few months after their loss. Even better, take them a meal and eat with them, or invite them to join you.

Just think about it ………….. if someone is suddenly left alone, how have the events of the day affected them? Is it a day when they may be desperate for some company or companionship?

Several months after my husband passed, a wicked prairie electrical storm came up one evening. I've had a fear of thunder and lightning since childhood and was huddled on my couch, terrified to move, as sheet lightning and wild winds raged around the yard. To my huge relief, one of my neighbours came along and said she just wondered if I might like some company. I felt like kissing her feet.

My husband and I always grew a large vegetable garden, which we enjoyed working in together. We had planted our usual massive garden the year he died. The task of cleaning up the garden that fall and dealing with all the produce by myself felt like an impossible task. I could not set foot in the garden by myself without being crushed with grief. One lovely fall day, I was surprised by many vehicles arriving in my yard as about ten friends showed up with enthusiasm, food and wine. They worked all day, completely cleaning up the garden and dispensing with the produce. After, we had a wonderful meal together. They **anticipated** the difficulty I had with dealing with the garden and they resolved it. I never would have asked anyone to help me with that task. It was a truly memorable day with wonderful friends.

- **Ask if there is something specific you can do to help**

- **Try to anticipate what the bereaved might need assistance with**

- **Food is universally helpful**

LIFELINE 8

CRISIS RESPONDERS & ENDURANCE COMPANIONS

MY FRIEND SILVIA MAINTAINS THAT THE ENTIRE SOCIAL construct of friendship is altered by grief. Within all our associations and social interactions, we assume roles. This friend is the comedian, that friend is the emotional counsellor, another friend is the social advisor and so on. Grief changes the social construct of our relationships. The grieving person is now different, and most likely will always be different. Many of us who have experienced tragic loss describe our lives in a before/after the loss fashion. Things are different now. We are different now. We do not relate to people the same way we once did. These may be subtle changes or more dramatic shifts in our personas. We may no longer be able to fulfill the role that we once had, and this can change relationships. Most people are waiting for us to get back to the way we were "before," and this may never occur.

When loss first occurs, typically many people rally around. In general, I think most people are "crisis responders." This is readily apparent in the outpouring of response when disaster strikes anywhere in the world. We line up to donate our money or our blood, household effects and food when tragedy strikes. We sign up to go on humanitarian missions to rebuild schools and medical centers. Once the current news bite fades, we are often quick to forget the ongoing needs of the disaster zone.

A very similar response happens when personal tragedy strikes. Often, in the aftermath of the immediate tragedy, many people reach out to help. This outreach of support is so appreciated, but we do, however, need people who will have the endurance to be long-term companions with us on the grief journey.

Not everyone can be this companion. Some close friends and associates may not be able to fulfill this role for many reasons. Some friends that you may have expected to be stalwart supporters just may not be able to provide that support. Others you least expected may step up in surprising ways.

Never underestimate the value of distant relationships and associations. I know of people who have said they were so touched by someone's situation but hesitated to step up as they were certain the person had closer friends and relatives who were supporting them. Do not make this assumption. I've had several people whom I barely knew prior to my husband's passing who have become very supportive friends. If you are touched by someone's loss, don't hesitate to reach out, regardless how peripheral your association. No one can have too much support, and you may be able to provide something that no one else can.

It takes truly special people to be able to go the distance with someone finding their way in grief. I feel that I held the feet of my family and friends to the fire of endurance as they allowed me to endlessly obsess over the loss of my husband. For years, I managed to turn almost every conversation into some discussion of his death. His death was my constant focus. One of the most difficult things with unexpected loss is reconciling our head and our heart to the reality of the person's death. We know cognitively that the person is gone, but our heart refuses to accept it. Some people are able to make this alignment and come to some **acceptance** of the loss sooner than others. By acceptance, I don't mean that they are ever okay with the loss; what I mean is that the loss has become "real." For many people, the loss is "unreal," and this sense of unreality creates a huge disconnect in their life for a very, very long time. It prevents people from being able to focus on anything else until they are able to come to the acceptance of this reality.

Shock puts us into an initial state of disbelief that can last for some time. When you finally get to the stage where your mind and your heart accept the reality of the loss, this can be a particularly devastating time. This is generally long after most people have forgotten that you are mourning and think you have "gotten over" grief. This is a time when people need all the support they can get.

I strongly urge people to be aware that this is a long, long road. It may be that the most useful thing you can do is pace your support. Think about reaching out to the person two months, four months, six months or a year after their loss. Their grief will still be very fresh to them. They will still need caring companions.

The pace of grief is like an endless dance marathon in which the set pattern can often feel like one step forward, two steps back. It's not fun for anyone. It's so much more enjoyable to be at the prom with the fun, cool kids than trudging through the unfamiliar steps of this melancholy tango with a sad partner. This is why we need a lot of dance partners. If you can sign someone's grief dance card, even once, it can go a long way to helping them keep moving their feet.

> - **No one person can do everything**
>
> - **Everyone can do something to help**

LIFELINE 9

BEWARE OF ELEPHANTS

I CANNOT STRESS ENOUGH HOW IMPORTANT IT IS TO **acknowledge** the cataclysmic loss that someone has experienced, no matter how much time has passed. The first time you see someone after their loss, please, please acknowledge it. If you hadn't seen or communicated with your friend Neil Armstrong until five years after his moon landing, you would still likely mention the fact that he had set foot on the moon. Life-altering, tragic loss is the bereaved person's moon landing. It will certainly become the elephant in the room if you don't mention it.

About six months after my husband passed away, I had two completely different social experiences that emphasize the point I'm making.

The first New Year's Eve after my husband passed, I was invited to a small get-together. I was struggling with the thought of facing a new year that my husband would never see and certainly did not feel that I could be around people celebrating. My dear friend encouraged me to try to go for a short while, with a promise to bring me home at any time that I wished to leave. As soon as we arrived, the host couple greeted me by saying, "We are so happy you came. We were just talking about the last time we got together with you and Gord." By immediately bringing Gord's name into the conversation, it put me completely at ease, and I was able to just be comfortable in the presence of good friends. By acknowledging that Gord was gone, it removed any perceived social obligation for me to act as if everything was completely normal. There was no need for me to put on my fake, "I'm okay, everything's fine" face. I will always be grateful for the ease I was put in by marvelous people who simply acknowledged my loss and allowed me to be very comfortable in the warmth of their friendship as the evening unfolded.

Around the same time, I was invited for dinner with two couples. One of the couples had not, and did not ever, acknowledge my husband's death in any way. It made for a very awkward evening. The conversation was stilted and superficial all evening as they tried to steer clear of any reference to the huge life change I had experienced. They clearly felt it would be taboo to mention my husband's death. I could hardly come up with any conversation that wouldn't reflect my new reality. It resulted in the "pressure cooker" effect, as I felt forced to put on my false "I'm okay" face. It was so difficult and felt so false that I simply couldn't wait to leave. It would have been so much easier for all of us if they had simply said, "We were so sorry to hear of your loss." That's all it takes. **Acknowledgement.** We would not have needed to continue talking about the tragic event, but it would shoo the elephant from the room, and we could continue on to other topics without fear of the conversation going in the wrong direction.

There are some people within my circle of community who have never acknowledged my husband's death to me. As a result, I've made up my own narrative about what they may be thinking. My husband died by suicide and, unfortunately, there is still stigma associated with that. I worry that they may have judged him in some way, which is disturbing to me. Chances are I'm completely off base with this guess as it is easy to conjure up scenarios at such a time. Chances are they simply didn't know what to say, so chose to say nothing. This is the cautionary tale. If you say nothing, people may make untrue assumptions. It is much wiser to acknowledge the loss. I repeat, just say "I'm so sorry for your loss."

- **Acknowledge the loss**

- **Always acknowledge the loss**

LIFELINE 10

GUILT VS. REGRET

IN ANY SITUATION OF LOSS, THERE ARE GENERALLY AMPLE feelings of guilt and regret to go around. Human nature tends to compel us to look to ourselves to assign blame. In the case of tragic, unexpected death, we are particularly inclined to think there may have been something that we could have done or should have done to prevent it.

- If only I had insisted he go to the doctor sooner

- If only I had said no to them attending that event

- If only I insisted on driving when I knew she was tired

- If only I'd seen how ill they were

- If only, if only, if only ....

All "if onlys" do is create a burden of guilt because we think we could have done something to change the outcome, but that is often not true.

Many losses that occur are a direct result of a decision or a number of decisions made by the person who has died. That is most certainly the case with suicide. Only one person makes the decision to take their life.

There is an expression in grief counselling for families who have lost someone to suicide that "you did the best that you could with the information that you had at the time." Of course, if we had any idea that someone was suicidal, we would move heaven and earth to prevent that outcome. For several years I've had a sign on my fridge that says: **"The WILL to save a life does not constitute the POWER to prevent a death."** This expression certainly applies to many more losses than suicide. This expression reminds us that we are not in control. The "if onlys" must be processed. They will not bring the person back and they create guilt which keeps us from finding stability and healing.

When we are prepared for someone's death, we have opportunity to say the things we wish to say and make amends if needed. This can greatly mitigate any residual regrets we may be left with.

When unexpected loss occurs, we have no such opportunity. We are often left with regret over any number of things.

I believe that we can learn to live with **regret**. **Guilt**, on the other hand, has the ability to destroy people's souls. It's very important for survivors to be able to distinguish between the two.

Guilt – a feeling of responsibility that you have specifically done something or failed to do something that you should have.

Regret – feeling of sadness or disappointment over something that has happened or been done.

I have many regrets around my husband's death that I will take to my grave. I was out of the country when he took his life. I had just arrived in Spain where I was going to be hiking a section of The Camino de Santiago for two weeks with some friends. The trip had been planned for a year, and my husband insisted that I go and was very enthusiastic about it. He assured me that he was fine, and it appeared that he was. He had many plans for interesting things he intended to do while I was away. I will always regret that I wasn't home and somehow able to intervene. I regret that I wasn't able to see how ill he was. I regret that the medical professionals that he did consult weren't able to see it either, and I especially regret that he was unable to articulate to anyone how desperate he felt. What I know now is that I have to name these things for what they are—**regrets**. I can and will have to live with those regrets forever. If I assume guilt for these things that were beyond my control, it will destroy me. Guilt has the soul-searing ability to destroy us mentally and physically.

In my personal grief journey, coming to understand the critical difference between guilt and regret was a watershed moment in my healing. It came about in a conversation I had with a family member who was close to my husband and had their own feelings of guilt over not being able to recognize the severity of his illness. I recall thinking how unwarranted his guilt feelings were because I knew without a doubt that given an opportunity, this family member would have done anything to help my husband. This realization held a magnifying glass to my own feelings. My absolute truth is I loved my husband as much as humanly possible and given a choice I would have done **anything** to prevent his death. Understanding that helps me to accurately name my feelings for what they are ……. REGRET.

If someone is feeling overwhelmed with feelings of guilt over things unspoken, or undone, or decisions made, it may well be that the most useful way to provide support may be to help them understand the difference between **guilt** and **regret**.

> - **The Will to save a life, does not constitute the Power to prevent a death**

LIFELINE 11

THE GREATEST GIFT

THE THING WE FEAR MOST WHEN WE'VE LOST SOMEONE WE love is that their lives will be forgotten or somehow deemed insignificant.

People are often reluctant to bring up a deceased person's name for a couple of generally misconceived notions:

1) "I don't want to say the person's name because it will remind the survivors of their death." Saying their name doesn't remind us of their **death,** it reminds us of their **life.**

2) "The survivor seems to be having a happy moment and appears to have momentarily forgotten the tragedy. I certainly don't want to remind them by bringing it up."

Believe me, we have not forgotten. Not for a second. Not even for a nano-second.

In *Bearing the Unbearable*, Joanne Cacciatore talks about the "constant presence of the absence." In my mind, no truer sentiment has ever been expressed. The absence of our loved one is always with us. Even if we seem happy, joyful or appear to be having fun, it is always with us. Not mentioning it does not make it less so. Mentioning our loved one is a wonderful gift at any time. It means that someone else is thinking of them, and they have not been forgotten.

My husband loved the sport of curling. About a year after he passed, I received a phone call from a lady who sometimes curled against him. She just randomly called me to say how much she missed seeing him at the curling rink. It was so wonderful. It made my day. I had a big cry after getting off the phone, but that was okay. I was so comforted by the thought that others still thought of him.

Sometimes when unexpected loss happens, the bereaved are left unable to even think about happy memories because it is just too painful. This leads to a fear that some memories may be forgotten about the person who is now gone. It's comforting to have confidence that others are holding on to wonderful memories. Someone once asked me "When is a good time to start talking about the deceased?" Immediately. Anytime is a good time.

Bringing the person's name into the conversation is especially heartwarming on special occasions and holidays. It's not morbid. The person who has passed is always on our minds, and when it's a special occasion, we are especially aware that they are missing it. When someone else brings them into the occasion by mentioning their name, it's like a warm hug. It's a very, very precious gift . . . please give generously.

- **It's a wonderful gift to mention the deceased person's name at any time**

- **Give generously!**

GOING
FORWARD

I CONSIDER MYSELF TO BE EXTREMELY FORTUNATE TO HAVE been living in a rural area when I lost my husband. I was surrounded by three caring communities where I basically knew everyone and had tremendous support. My children live two provinces away from me. When they were getting ready to return home after my husband's funeral, they were, of course, worried about the fact that they were a long distance from me. A lovely lady in the community said to them, "I know you're concerned that your mom is alone. Don't worry. We've got this. As a community, we've got this." That statement went a long way to easing my children's minds. They knew I had an incredible support system. I think often of people who experience tragic losses in more isolated situations, and their road would be much more difficult than mine. Sometimes people who live in cities have a more limited base of personal associations, and it is easy for people to assume that someone else is providing care and support.

My thoughts have come from my personal perspective of losing my husband. He was well-liked and respected by all who knew him. Most people saw his death as the tragic loss that it was. The fact that his death was from suicide, which is often greatly misunderstood, resulted in some people being uncertain and uncomfortable with expressing sympathy.

There are many losses that we simply do not understand. There are many losses where the circumstances of the loss clouds our ability to respond. Some examples might be people who have lost infants, missing persons, domestic murders, or youth who are killed while involved in some illegal activity, just to name a few. Behind all those losses is a family that is grieving. We do not need to judge a situation that we don't understand. The salient point is that people left behind are suffering and require support in the same way as anyone else who has experienced loss. Small kindnesses can go a long way in helping people endure their loss.

At the time of writing this, our world is in the grips of the novel Covid 19 pandemic. It is too early to speculate on what change this pandemic will bring to our world as we knew it before 2020. We do know that some things will be permanently changed, and there will be losses, both large and small, that people will grieve. We will experience global grief on some level, and now, more than ever, we need to lean into acknowledgment of each other's grief in order to care for each other. Now more than ever, it is essential that we intentionally bear witness to each other's pain.

There is no magic formula in the preceding chapters. These are simply some basic suggestions for helping people to feel more confidence in going forward to comfort others when they are called to do so. Mostly, these are ideas that you already knew, but you may have just had a little uncertainty about whether your instincts were right. Grief is not a taboo subject for those of us who have experienced it, but it is difficult and uncomfortable for those who haven't. It takes courage to enter into someone else's pain and anguish, and even more courage to remain there. Doing and saying something is **always** better than doing and saying nothing. Your actions, large and small, will have a huge impact on helping someone endure the unimaginable.

Grief has changed my life forever. There is not a day that I don't miss my husband and long for his presence, but I refuse to allow the burden of grief to define me. Life is precious. I will live into my years by having a joyful, meaningful life for both of us. It will not, however, be without the bottomless regret that he is not able to live it with me.

Don't be afraid of grief. Eventually we will all experience it, one way or another.

- **Be brave**
- **Reach out**
- **Don't worry about what to say**
- **Do something useful**
- **Always acknowledge the loss**
- **Never hesitate to mention the person's name**
- **Be kind**
- **Be very, very patient**

No one can make tragic loss less devastating, but everyone can do something to make it endurable.

APPENDIX 1

SUICIDE

SINCE MY HUSBAND'S DEATH BY SUICIDE, I CONSIDER IT TO be one of my most important life purposes to bring as much awareness as possible to mental illness. While there is growing awareness of mental illness and suicide, there is still so much that we just don't know.

Generally, we can all understand when death occurs from physical illness. We also understand that there is a randomness in our universe in which tragic accidents occur. We know that random or intentional acts of violence happen to innocent people. These things are all terribly tragic losses.

One of the problems with suicide is that a healthy mind simply cannot comprehend how anyone could make the decision to take their own life. Therefore, we have a tendency to compartmentalize suicides in a way that we can understand. We've all heard people say, "Well, that person who took their life had a problem with addictions, or they had relationship problems or financial problems." Certainly, some of these things may have been present in that person's life, but millions of people in the world have these issues but don't end their lives. That takes an additional affliction, which is generally the disease of mental illness.

Certainly, it was the question that people asked me the most when my husband took his life. "Why did he do it?" It is inconceivable for people to understand how anyone who has a wonderful life and everything to live for could possibly make this decision. People were waiting for the aha! moment—the moment when they would find out he had some secret addiction, a dire physical diagnosis, or some other catastrophic circumstance. His death was a huge shock to everyone who knew him because he had none of these.

Mental illness can cover a wide range of afflictions, but a common denominator is typically some sort of chemical imbalance in the brain. Sometimes that imbalance can be treated, and sometimes that imbalance becomes terminal. Most people who end their lives do not want to die, but they desperately want to end their pain; pain that has become completely unbearable to them. Suicide becomes a reasonable option for people when the thought of enduring another day of their mental anguish far exceeds any fear they have of death.

I once took a training course that had a component on working with people with mental health issues. A classmate was adamant that he would not work with anyone who appeared suicidal. He would be passing them on to someone else who had more expertise in this area. This begged the question of how he would know they were suicidal. He was certain that there would be obvious signs. While it is true that there sometimes are red flags, often there are not, or the signs are so subtle they are only identifiable in hindsight.

We have a notion that we can recognize depression, because sometimes we can. We all know people who wear their depression on their sleeves. We know they are struggling, and when these people see suicide as their only option, we are sometimes not completely shocked. We've witnessed their struggle.

What I now know (that I wish I had known years ago) was that my husband suffered from "high functioning depression," also known as persistent depressive disorder. My opinion, and this is strictly my opinion, is that most people who suffer from depression are just like my husband. To the world, they appear to be completely fine. They are very functional. Their battle is entirely internal. They are doing everything they can to function normally without allowing anyone to see the anguish they are in.

What shocked me after my husband's death was the sheer number of people who said to me, "You know, I've been on anti-depressants for twelve years. But please don't tell anyone." I can guarantee you that these people are your neighbours, your friends and your family members, and their number is much higher than you can imagine.

A Major Depressive Episode, is categorized as a feeling of being down for two weeks or more. If a person experiences one Major Depressive Episode, they are 50% likely to have another Major Depressive Episode. After two episodes, they are 70% likely to have another, and after three episodes, they are 90% likely to have more[1]. It is no wonder these people feel that the way they are feeling will never, ever end. This constant struggle to function and appear normal during these increasing down spells must be completely exhausting and overwhelming. It's also easy to see how we overlook it. We all have spells when we feel down from time to time, and we don't always tell anyone how we feel.

Then how can we respond to someone who is struggling?

A few years ago, if someone showed up on my doorstep and said they were feeling down, I would have been hugely sympathetic. I would have invited them in, put the coffee on, served them some cookies and tried to cheer them up, because this is what we do in rural Saskatchewan. And while we need to talk, talk, talk about mental illness, we also need to be fearless in these conversations. We need to ask people specifically what they are doing to get help. If they are not getting the help they need, we need to definitely assist them in seeking additional help. We need

---

1   American Psychiatric Association (2000) *Diagnostic and Statistical Manual of Mental Disorders* (4th ed. text revision) Washington (DC): Author, pp.341-2

to ask if they have thoughts of suicide, and we need to actually say that terrible word. In my mind, it is NOT helpful terminology to ask someone if they are thinking of hurting themselves. To someone whose mind has been altered by a chemical imbalance, suicide is not necessarily seen as hurting themselves; rather, it can be seen as a sensible solution to ending pain. **Mental Health professionals affirm it does not make a person suicidal by asking them.**

I've spent a lot of time thinking about what could have saved my husband. This, of course, is the extreme hell of suicide. Everyone who is left behind feels that they should have been able to see how ill he was and that they should have been able to intervene in some manner. The reality is that people can only see what they are allowed to see and can only intervene if they know what someone is intending. (See Lifeline # 10) The answer to what might have helped is this: If he had only been able to articulate to someone how desperate he was feeling, it may have changed the outcome.

Depression is similar an auto-immune disease in which the body attacks itself. A depressed mind is constantly giving the person messages that they are weak, helpless, and they are never going to feel any better than they do right now. How, then, can someone in this mindset speak up when there is still so much stigma attached to mental illness? We desperately need to normalize this terrible illness. We would not think any less of someone who had disease in any of their other organs. If someone is on thyroid medication, we do not judge them. Why would we judge someone on medication for disease that just happens to be in a different organ? That organ is their brain.

We need to create an environment where people can self-disclose without fear of stigma. We need to make it easier for people who are struggling to reach out, and there needs to be far more resources available for help.

A recent study showed that over a three-year period, 35% of the adult population had consulted a physician for a mental health problem[2]. This is one of those drop-in-a-bucket statistics because of the many people who suffer on their own without seeking medical help. Depending on which statistic you are using, one in three or one in five

---

2   Martens, P. Fransoo, R. Mckeen, N, et al (2004) *Patterns of regional mental illness disorder diagnoses and services use in Manitoba: a population based study.* Winnipeg (MB): Manitoba Centre for Health Policy., p.28

people will have a mental health issue in their lifetime. Either way, that is a staggering number that essentially affects all of us.

Mental health is underfunded at all levels. We need far more funding for mental health to make significant changes. If you are looking for a place to make your charitable donations impact virtually everyone you know, mental health is a good place to start.

Most of all, we need to educate ourselves about this disease. We need to banish the myth that mental illness is some sort of personal weakness that people have somehow chosen and that we can help cheer them up or help them "get a grip".

We can all be part of the change by being part of the conversation.

APPENDIX 2

EVERY HEALTH REGION HAS GOVERNMENT MENTAL HEALTH resources as well as numerous professionals who can assist people suffering from mental illness.

The following is a list of some Canadian resources for more information:

Canadian Mental Health Assoc. (CMHA)
Phone: 613-745-7750

National Network for Mental
Health (PMDA)
http://ppda.ca

Mood Disorders Society of Canada
Phone: 613-921-5565
http://www.mdsc.ca

The Lifeline Canada Foundation
http: thelifelinecanada.ca

Anxiety Canada
http://www.anxietycanada.ca/

Kids Help Phone
Phone: 1-800-668-6868
https://kidshelpphone.ca/

ACKNOWLEDGEMENTS

I WILL BE ETERNALLY THANKFUL TO THE LEGIONS OF family, friends and community who comforted, supported and journeyed with me and continue to accompany me as I find my way. You know who you are. Thank you, thank you, thank you!!

Thank you to my friends Irene Gareau, Catherine Barnsley and Rick McCorrister who were early readers of my manuscript. I am extremely grateful for your thoughtful feedback and invaluable editorial suggestions.

Thank you to my children Crystal and Cory who have been on this journey with me. Your ongoing love, support and encouragement enabled me to get Sincere Condolences to the finish line.

ABOUT THE
AUTHOR

JOYCE AITKEN BRINGS COMPASSION, WISDOM AND WIT TO her work as an author, speaker and advocate for grief and mental health awareness. Since her retirement as an urban municipal CAO she volunteers at a Palliative Care unit and with a variety of grief organizations. A lifelong resident of Saskatchewan "Land of the Living Skies", she has lived in northern and southern Saskatchewan and now makes her home in Saskatoon.

joyaitken@sasktel.net

www.sincerecondolences.ca

Lightning Source UK Ltd.
Milton Keynes UK
UKHW011417240621
386089UK00001B/302